DINO DETECTIVE

IN TRAINING

KINGFISHER

DINOSAUR ACADEMY

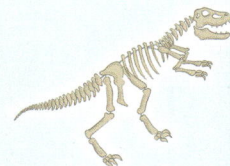

TRAINING PROGRAMME

Theory 1: **Training Time** 6

Practical 1: **Dinosaur Detective's Kit** 8

Theory 2: **The Time of the Dinosaurs** 10

Theory 3: **Drifting Continents** 12

Practical 2: **What's a Fossil?** 14

Practical 3: **Other Kinds of Fossil** 16

Practical 4: **Rock Solid** 18

Practical 5: **Fossil Hunting** 20

Practical 6: **Where in the World?** 22

Theory 4: **Mesozoic Animals** 24

Theory 5: **All Kinds of Dinosaurs** 26

Theory 6: **Meat-eating Dinosaurs** 28

DINOSAUR ACADEMY

DINO DETECTIVE

IN TRAINING

DINOSAUR ACADEMY

STUDENT PASS

Name ....

KINGFISHER

First published 2021 by Kingfisher
an imprint of Macmillan Children's Books
The Smithson. 6 Briset Street. London EC1M 5NR
Associated companies throughout the world
www.panmacmillan.com

Author: Tracey Turner
Series editor: Kathryn Jewitt
Designer: Jeni Child

ISBN 978-0-75344599-0
Copyright © Macmillan Publishers International Ltd 2021

9 8 7 6 5 4 3 2 1

1TR/1220/WKT/UG/128MA

A CIP catalogue record for this book is available from the British Library.

Printed in China

Picture credits
The Publisher would like to thank the following for permission to reproduce their material.
Top = t: Bottom = b: Centre = c: Left = l: Right = r
iStock: 18t Moorefam. 18b raciro. 19br hsvrs. 19tr fotoVoyager. 19tl Preto_perola. 19bl fmajor 21 tacojim. 22b
zrfphoto: Shutterstock: 15 Elenarts. 20 NorthStarPhotos. 22–23t Ian Woolcock. 22–23c Pyty. 26–27aekky.
28 DenysHolovaituk. 36–37 Elenamiv. 39t Sara Kadrijevic. 39b Sanit Fuangnakhon.

Theory 7: **Dinosaur Defences** 30

Theory 8: **Giant Dinosaurs**........................ 32

Theory 9: **Sea Creatures** 34

Theory 10: **Flying Reptiles** 36

Practical 7: **The End of the Dinosaurs** 38

Practical 8: **Get Digging** 40

Hall of fame 42

Examination 44

Dinosaur speak 46

Answers 48

THEORY

PRACTICAL

THEORY pages are full of important information that you need to know.

PRACTICAL pages have a task to do or a dinosaur detective skill to acquire. Tick each page when you have completed that part of your training.

TRAINING TIME

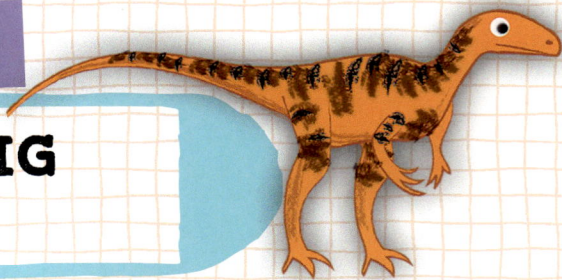

So, you want to be a dinosaur detective? Do you love finding out about prehistoric creatures? Are you good at working out clues? Then congratulations! Your training starts today.

Dinosaurs died out millions of years ago (MYA), so dinosaur detectives have to hunt for the clues that dinosaurs and other prehistoric creatures left behind: fossils. But the job isn't just about digging things up . . .

YOU WILL NEED TO . . .

Study hard and learn a LOT about dinosaurs and other prehistoric living things.

Find out about how planet Earth has changed, and different kinds of rock, to discover where fossils are likely to be found.

Examine existing fossils, so that you can compare and contrast new fossils with ones that have already been found.

Can you find the dinosaur egg on each page?

Use tools to excavate rock and find fossils.

Employ your detective skills to identify what you find.

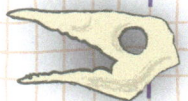

Present your results to other dinosaur detectives and other kinds of scientists.

ACTIVITY

Can you guess which of these items are used by a dinosaur detective?

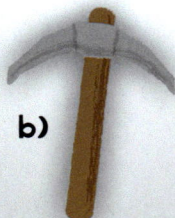

a)

b)

c)

d)

e)

f)

g)

h)

PRACTICAL 1

DINOSAUR DETECTIVE'S KIT

Dinosaur detectives need special kit to help them do their job. Before you start your training, make sure you have everything you need.

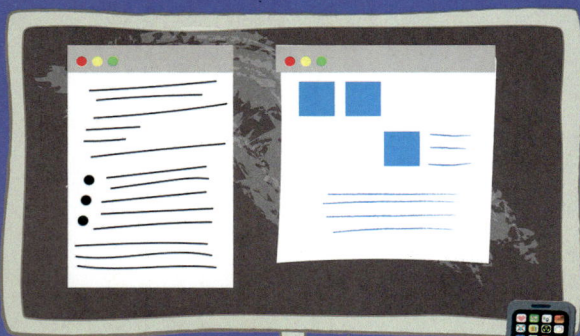

CLOTHING

You'll need to dress for detecting success:

○ practical, hard-wearing clothes

○ sturdy boots for difficult terrain

○ a hi-vis jacket so you are easy to spot

○ a hard hat to protect your head on a dig, especially if you're near a cliff face

CHECKLIST

Can you spot these things in the big picture?

- ☐ Hammer and chisel to excavate your finds
- ☐ Picks and probes for prodding and scraping
- ☐ Brushes for dusting off the fossils you uncover
- ☐ Spade and trowel for digging
- ☐ Binoculars to scan for suitable sites
- ☐ Goggles to protect your eyes from rock splinters and dust
- ☐ Magnifying glass to examine your finds closely
- ☐ Notebook and pen to record your finds
- ☐ Tape measure and ball of string to take measurements

KIT BAG

Always take a strong bag to carry any fossils you unearth. You also need to take some tissue paper or bubble wrap to protect your finds.

THE TIME OF THE DINOSAURS

Are you ready to travel millions of years back in time? That's when dinosaurs stalked our planet. Different kinds came and went, along with many other creatures.

THE MESOZOIC ERA

The time of the dinosaurs is also known as the Mesozoic Era. It started when the first dinosaurs appeared, about 240 million years ago, and ended 66 million years ago, when the dinosaurs died out.

The Mesozoic Era is divided into three periods:

THEORY NO: 2
tick here
APPROVED

240–201 MILLION YEARS AGO

Plateosaurus

Eoraptor

TRIASSIC PERIOD

The first ever dinosaurs appeared during the Triassic. The climate was hot and dry, and plant life included conifers (like today's fir trees) and ferns.

Triassic dinosaurs included:
Eoraptor, a small meat-eating dinosaur
Plateosaurus, a 7-m-long plant-eater

Diplodocus

JURASSIC PERIOD

201–145 MILLION YEARS AGO

The climate was still warm during the Jurassic period, but not as dry. There were lots of plants, and some enormous plant-eating dinosaurs!

Jurassic dinosaurs included:
Diplodocus, a HUGE 26-m-long plant-eater
Stegosaurus, an armoured 9-m-long dinosaur

Stegosaurus

CRETACEOUS PERIOD

145–66 MILLION YEARS AGO

The first flowers bloomed during the Cretaceous period. There were more different kinds of dinosaur than ever before, as well as many other animals.

Cretaceous dinosaurs included:
Tyrannosaurus, a 12-m-long meat-eater
Iguanodon, a 10-m-long plant-eater

Iguanodon

Tyrannosaurus

END OF THE DINOSAURS

ACTIVITY

Match each dinosaur to the correct time period.

a) Diplodocus
b) Iguanodon
c) Eoraptor

1. Triassic
2. Jurassic
3. Cretaceous

DRIFTING CONTINENTS

It might seem as though the land on Earth always stays in one place, but actually the Earth's crust is made up of gigantic plates that are moving very slowly. When the dinosaurs were alive, the Earth looked very different from how it does today. As a dinosaur detective, you'll need to know how it has changed.

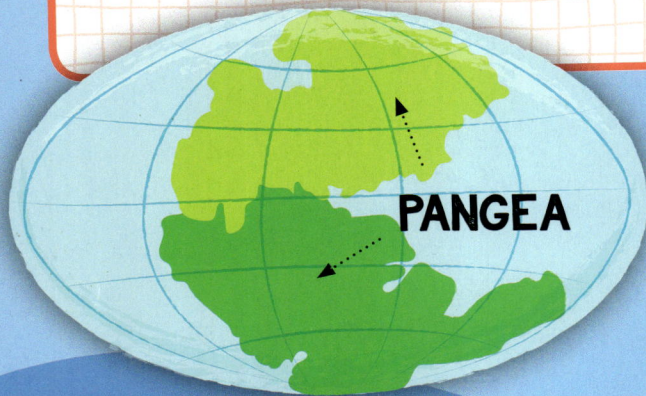

PANGEA

LAURASIA

GONDWANA

PANGEA

JURASSIC

At the beginning of the age of the dinosaurs, during the Triassic, all the Earth's land was joined together in one big continent called Pangea.

During the Jurassic, the huge continent of land started to divide in two. There were two main continents – Laurasia in the north and Gondwana in the south, separated by the Tethys Sea.

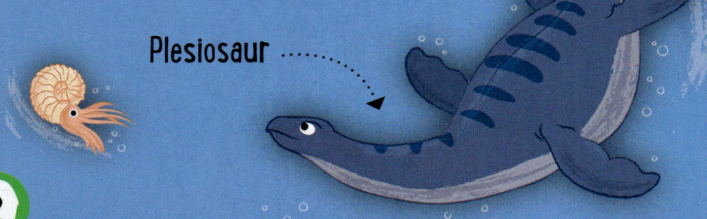

Plesiosaur

Ichthyosaur

WORK IT OUT ...

Fossils can show how continents have moved. For example, fossils of a reptile called Mesosaurus were found only in South America and in Africa – either the land was once joined, or Mesosaurus could swim across the sea or fly – it was a freshwater animal, and it didn't have wings!

Mesosaurus

THEORY NO: 3
tick here
APPROVED

ACTIVITY

The coasts of west Africa and east South America look as though they fit together like puzzle pieces. Once upon a time, they did! Can you spot South America and Africa on a map of the world, and work out where they were in the time of the dinosaurs?

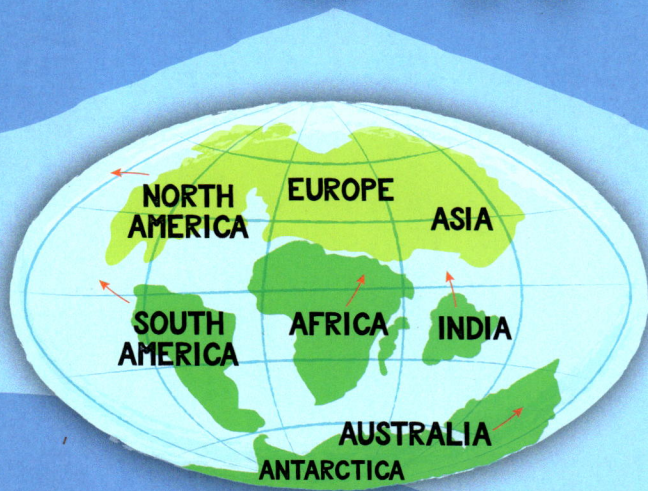

NORTH AMERICA · EUROPE · ASIA
SOUTH AMERICA · AFRICA · INDIA
AUSTRALIA
ANTARCTICA

NORTH AMERICA · EUROPE · ASIA
SOUTH AMERICA · AFRICA · INDIA
AUSTRALIA
ANTARCTICA

CRETACEOUS

By the Cretaceous, the continents had drifted further apart, more like they are today. The sea level was higher, though, and North America and Africa were both split down the middle by sea, while Europe and Asia were broken up into islands.

Mosasaur

TODAY

Today, the continents are still moving. About 250 million years from now, the continents could be back in one supercontinent again!

Hybodus

WHAT'S A FOSSIL?

Fossils are the remains that prehistoric plants and animals left behind. They are how we know dinosaurs and other animals existed, and they give lots of clues about what these creatures were like when they were alive. Let's dig one up and take a closer look.

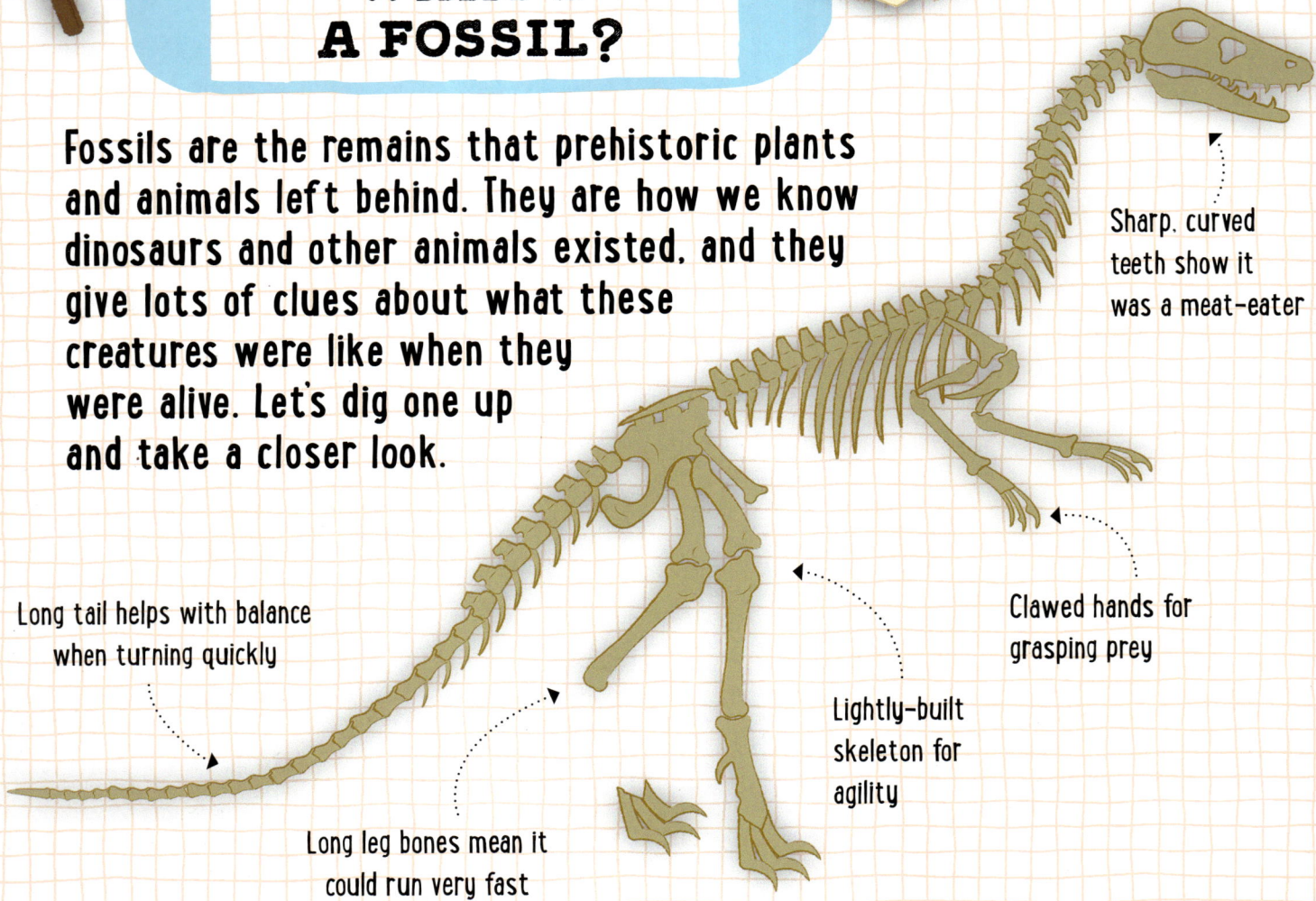

Sharp, curved teeth show it was a meat-eater

Long tail helps with balance when turning quickly

Clawed hands for grasping prey

Lightly-built skeleton for agility

Long leg bones mean it could run very fast

ACTIVITY

When you find fossilized bones it is not always easy to tell which part goes where, or which bones fit together. Which of these bones is the missing part of this Compsognathus fossil?

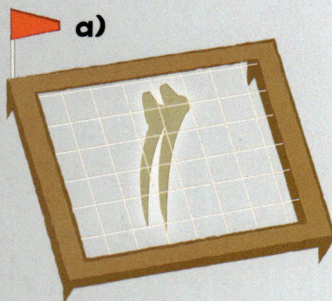

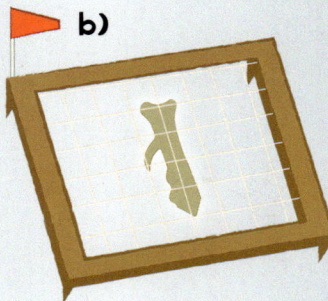

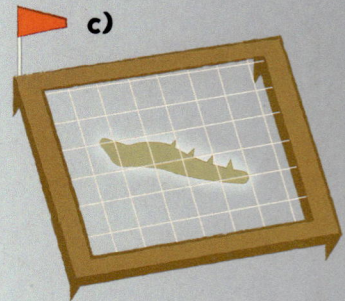

a)

b)

c)

HOW IS A FOSSIL MADE?

1 The dinosaur died, fell into a river and became buried in the soft mud at the bottom.

2 The soft body parts rotted away over time. The hard teeth and bones were covered by more mud and sand.

3 The mud turned into rock. Water seeped into the teeth and bones and left minerals behind, turning them into hard stone.

4 Over millions of years, the landscape changed completely. What was once a riverbed is now a cliff face.

5 A rock slide exposed the fossilized dinosaur skeleton just in time for you to find it!

LUCKY FIND
Very few animals turned into fossils because conditions have to be just right. So you're very lucky to find one!

This is Compsognathus (comp-sog-nathus), a small dinosaur from the Jurassic Period.

PRACTICAL NO: 2
tick here
APPROVED

15

Dinosaur tracks in mud hardened over millions of years to preserve them. The prints can tell us a lot about the size, type, weight and even the speed of the dinosaur.

Stegosaurus

Ankylosaurus

OTHER KINDS OF FOSSIL

As well as fossilized bones and teeth, dinosaurs left behind other clues for detectives to find. These "trace fossils" give us a glimpse into the past.

Some prehistoric animals made burrows that became preserved in rock.

DINO POO!

Fossilized dinosaur poo is known as coprolite. It can tell us about what the animal ate.

Iguanodon

Very occasionally, the imprint of a prehistoric animal's skin or feathers might be preserved as a fossil. This is how dinosaur detectives first found out that some dinosaurs had feathers, and others had scaly skin.

Trails are impressions left by animals that slithered along, such as prehistoric snakes.

ACTIVITY

Follow the tracks to see which dinosaur made them!

a)    b)   c)

START HERE

ROCK SOLID

Scientists divide the rocks in the Earth's crust into three main groups. It's a dinosaur detective's job to know about them, because then you'll know where to look for fossils.

granite

IGNEOUS ROCKS

These rocks form when super-hot liquid rock underneath the Earth's crust cools and hardens. This can happen when a volcano erupts and lava shoots out, or it can happen under the ground. It's very unlikely to contain fossils.

basalt

Fill in the missing letters to complete these types of rock. Which one might contain fossils?

○1. _RA_IT_ ○2. LI_E_TO_E ○3. G_EI__

gneiss (say 'nice')

sandstone

METAMORPHIC ROCKS

These rocks are made under extreme pressure or high temperatures, when other rocks are squashed or heated deep underground. It's very unlikely that a fossil could survive all that heat or squashing.

marble

SEDIMENTARY ROCKS

These rocks are made from very tiny pieces of rock that fell to the bottom of the sea (or a lake or river). Over a long period of time, the pieces were squished together to form rocks. Sedimentary rocks are where you are most likely to find fossils!

limestone

PRACTICAL NO: 4
tick here
APPROVED

19

FOSSIL HUNTING

How does a dinosaur detective track down fossils when they've been buried inside rock for millions of years? Grab your hammer and chisel and let's find out.

RAISED ROCKS

Sometimes, the Earth's plates bump into one another, pushing rock upwards, and, if you're lucky, revealing fossils. Over a long period of time, a really big bump can form mountains! That's why sea animal fossils can be found on mountain tops. Rocks can also be pushed to the surface when new rock forms underneath them, or when ice sheets melt.

WILD WEATHER

Rain, frost and wind can wear away rock over time. This is especially true of sedimentary rock, where fossils are found. A mountainside can suddenly reveal its fossil treasures after a bad storm. A landslide can expose hidden fossils too.

DIGGING DEEP

Fossils can also be revealed when people carve through hillsides to build roads, or make underground tunnels.

A RARE FIND

Finding a whole fossilized bone is rare, and finding a whole fossilized skeleton is rarer still! Dinosaur detectives have to be patient. Never give up, because one day you might make a world famous discovery!

KEEP A LOOKOUT

Once you've found the right type of rock that's the right age, you need to use your observational skills to look closely and carefully. If you find what look like small bone fragments, that could be a sign there's a fossil close by.

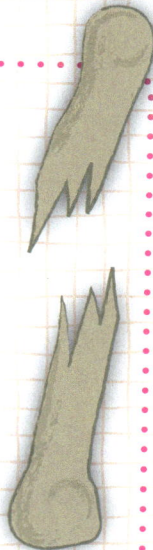

ACTIVITY

Look at these shapes – which ones look like they might be fossils?

PRACTICAL NO: 5

tick here

APPROVED

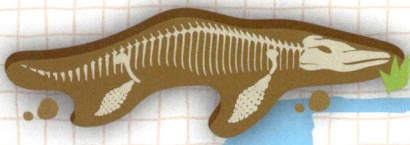

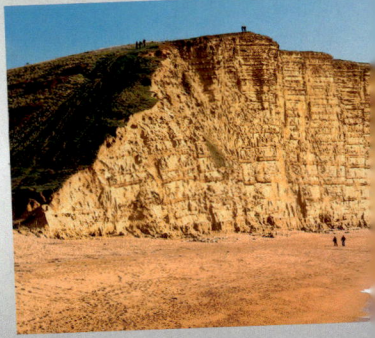

WHERE IN THE WORLD?

Fossils have been found on all of the world's continents, so dinosaur detectives might need to travel all over the world in search of them.

HOW OLD?

Fossils date from Earth's early history, billions of years ago, to recent discoveries thousands of years old. (To dinosaur scientists, something thousands of years old is very young!) The fossils you're interested in date from the Mesozoic Era, the time of the dinosaurs. Here are three of the best places on Earth to find them.

NORTH AMERICA

Hell Creek

SOUTH AMERICA

HELL CREEK, USA

The rocks of Hell Creek span Wyoming, North and South Dakota and Montana. They contain fossils from the Late Cretaceous, including the famous dinosaurs Tyrannosaurus, Triceratops and Ankylosaurus, as well as many other plant and animal fossils from the time of the dinosaurs.

JURASSIC COAST, UK

This Dorset coastline is 152 km long and has cliffs and rocks containing fossils from the whole of the Mesozoic Era. Fossils of the armoured dinosaur Scelidosaurus have been found here, along with dinosaur tracks, sea creatures such as plesiosaurs and ichthyosaurs, and plenty of ammonites – which look a bit like flat sea snails.

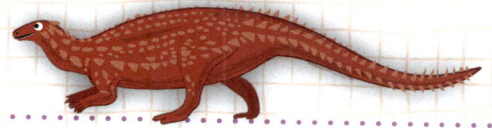

EUROPE

Dorset

ASIA

Sichuan

AFRICA

PRACTICAL NO: 6

tick here

APPROVED

How many dinosaurs can you spot on this map?

AUSTRALIA

SHAXIMIAO FORMATION, CHINA

The rocks in the Shaximiao formation of Sichuan have revealed more than 20 different kinds of dinosaur from the Jurassic Period, including huge plant-eating sauropods, as well as other Jurassic creatures. The dinosaur museum in the nearby city of Zigong has one of the highest number of dinosaur fossils found anywhere in the world!

WHAT'S A DINOSAUR?

Dinosaurs were land animals. There were different kinds, but they all had hip bones that meant they could stand and walk upright. Many were good runners, which gave dinosaurs an advantage against some other kinds of animal. All dinosaurs hatched from eggs.

THEORY 4

MESOZOIC ANIMALS

Dinosaurs weren't the only animals in the world during the Mesozoic Era. There were other creatures on land, in the air and in the sea.

Furry little mammals like this Morganucodon first appeared in the time of the dinosaurs.

LAND ANIMALS

Some prehistoric reptiles like Dimetrodon looked similar to dinosaurs, but they had legs that splayed out to the sides. Dimetrodon is actually more closely related to humans than to dinosaurs! Other land animals included our own ancestors, mammals.

THEORY NO: 4
tick here
APPROVED

FLYING REPTILES

Pterosaurs swooped and dived through the skies, catching insects and fish. Some were as small as seagulls, but the biggest was the size of a small aeroplane. Find out more on pages 36–37.

SEA CREATURES

Different types of sea creature swam in the oceans, such as ichthyosaurs, plesiosaurs, ammonites and mosasaurs. Find out more on pages 34–35.

ACTIVITY

Which one of these animals is a dinosaur?

○ Pteranodon

○ Morganucodon

○ Velociraptor

○ Plesiosaur

ALL KINDS OF DINOSAURS

Dinosaurs lived for many millions of years, so it's no surprise that there were more than a thousand different kinds, and new ones are discovered all the time. Here are just a few.

COELOPHYSIS

This dinosaur lived during the Triassic, and was one of the earliest meat-eating dinosaurs. It was about 2 m long, fast and agile, and ate lizards and insects. The biggest predators at the time weren't dinosaurs but big reptiles called rauisuchids (rah-i-soo-chid) and phytosaurs (figh-to-saws).

MICRORAPTORS

Some of the smallest dinosaurs were microraptors, which lived around 125 million years ago, during the Cretaceous. They were only about 1 kg in weight – the size of a crow. They had feathers and some kinds could probably fly or glide. They preyed on animals such as lizards and mammals.

PARASAUROLOPHUS

Some dinosaurs had impressive head crests, like Parasaurolophus (para-saw-olo-fus). It belonged to a group of plant-eating dinosaurs with beaks, called hadrosaurs. The dinosaur was 11 m long and lived in the Cretaceous period. The bony crest on its head might have been used to make loud, booming calls.

ACTIVITY

Spot the five differences between these two dinosaurs. What kind of dinosaur are they?

THEORY NO: 5
tick here
APPROVED

Scientists can use fossils to recreate lifelike models of dinosaurs. Can you match each dinosaur in the museum to the right description below?

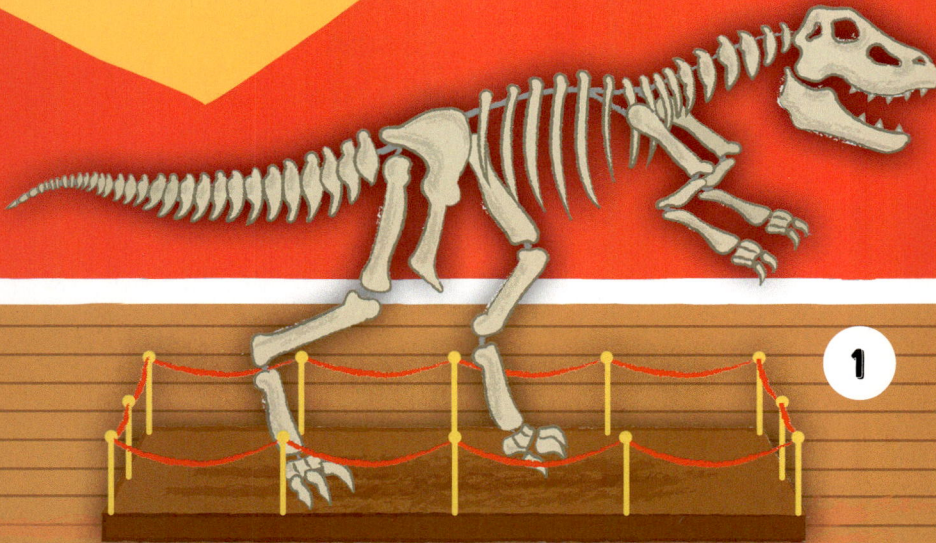

THEORY NO: 6

tick here

APPROVED

1

THEORY 6

MEAT-EATING DINOSAURS

Think of a dinosaur and you probably imagine something enormous with sharp teeth. Let's take a close look at three meat-eating dinosaurs.

SPINOSAURUS

- Lived during Cretaceous Period, about 112–97 MYA
- Size: 18 m long (largest meat-eater on Earth but not the heaviest)
- Weight: 6.5 tonnes
- Long, bony sail on its back and a long, narrow crocodile-like head

Spinosaurus only left behind a few fossilized bones, so scientists had to do a lot of detective work to piece together a picture of its size and shape.

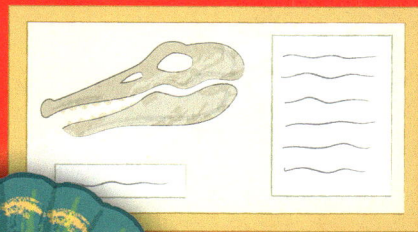

TYRANNOSAURUS REX

- Lived during Cretaceous Period, 68–66 MYA
- Size: 12 m long
- Weight: 7 tonnes
- 60 saw-edged teeth up to 20 cm long

Probably the most famous dinosaur of all. We know about it from around 30 T-rex fossils found in western North America. Some are almost complete skeletons. Bone fragments in its fossilized dung tell us that it could crush bone with its powerful jaws and teeth.

GIGANOTOSAURUS

- Lived in Cretaceous Period, about 112–90 MYA
- Size: 13.2 m long
- Weight: 7 tonnes
- 3 fingers on hands (T-rex had 2)

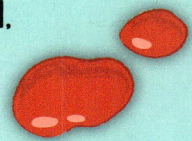

Like Spinosaurus, this dinosaur left behind just a few bones, but experts were able to work out a lot from them. By measuring a thigh bone's width and length, they can make a good guess at the dinosaur's weight. If they find a lot of the backbone, it's a big clue to the length of the dinosaur.

DINOSAUR DEFENCES

Now you know about some of the ferocious meat-eaters who preyed on other dinosaurs. These plant-eating dinosaurs evolved ways of defending themselves against predators like T-rex.

ANKYLOSAURUS

Ankylosaurus was a 7-m-long armoured dinosaur covered in bony plates. It had an extra tough skull and a bony club on the end of its tail that it could use to bash predators. Ankylosaurus lived during the Late Cretaceous.

MATCH UP!

Can you match each of these dino defences with the dinosaurs on this page?

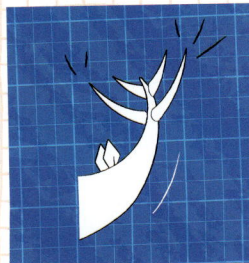
a)

b)

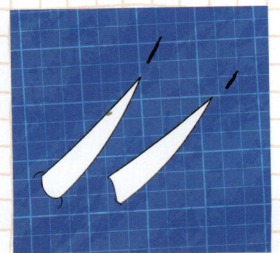
c)

TRICERATOPS

Triceratops was a 9-m-long plant-eater that lived in the Late Cretaceous. It had three long, sharp horns to fight off predators, and a tough frill around its neck for protection.

A Triceratops fossil shows a missing horn with bite marks that match Tyrannosaurus teeth – the fossil showed the horn had healed, so that Triceratops must have survived the fight!

STEGOSAURUS

Stegosaurus swung its spiky tail to defend itself against Late Jurassic dinosaurs such as the huge meat-eating Allosaurus.

No one really knows what the big bony plates on its back were for, but they might have been a scary signal to warn predators away. Although it was 9 m long, Stegosaurus had a small head and a brain the size of a plum!

THEORY NO: 7
tick here
APPROVED

Being big also meant these giant beasts could reach and eat leaves in the tallest trees.

GIANT DINOSAURS

Some plant-eating dinosaurs grew so big that no predator would attack them. They lived mainly during the Jurassic Period.

Diplodocus was a sauropod, a group of dinosaurs that includes the largest land animals ever. They walked on four legs and had very long necks and tails. Their heads were small compared to their enormous bodies.

ACTIVITY

Can you spot two different things in the picture that could one day become trace fossils?

As well as being too big for predators to attack, some sauropods had whip-like tails that they could lash at attackers.

Diplodocus lived 155-145 MYA. It was 26 m long - the length of three buses!

THEORY NO: 8

tick here

APPROVED

RARE FIND

Dinosaur hunters were lucky enough to find an almost complete fossilized Diplodocus skeleton in Wyoming, USA.

Dinosaur detectives think that these massive plant-eaters swallowed stones to help them digest the tough plants they ate.

Plesiosaurs looked a bit like a scary swimming diplodocus, but with flippers instead of legs. They were fierce meat-eaters.

Ichthyosaurs were sea reptiles that looked like dolphins. In fact, they weren't related to marine mammals or to fish, and died out completely.

SEA CREATURES

It's time to find out about some of the animals that lived in the sea while dinosaurs stomped about on land.

AMMONITES

Ammonites are common fossils today. Some were tiny, but others were bigger than you are. Their shells were a flat spiral made up of chambers. They were relatives of today's squid and octopus.

Mosasaurs were terrifying predators, a bit like a cross between a giant sea snake and a crocodile!

THEORY NO: 9
tick here
APPROVED

Different kinds of shark have lived on Earth for more than 400 million years. This one, called hybodus, swam in Mesozoic seas.

FOSSILS OF SEA CREATURES

Animals that lived in water were more likely to become fossils than land animals, so there are many more sea creature fossils than there are dinosaur fossils.

Can you identify the sea creature from this fossil?

FLYING REPTILES

Pterosaurs swooped through Mesozoic skies. They first appeared around 210 million years ago and died out completely at the same time as the dinosaurs. Here are four of these flying reptiles:

QUETZALCOATLUS

Pronunciation: quet-zal-co-atlus
Lived: 72-66 million years ago
Where: North America
Wingspan: more than 10 m
Diet: crayfish and dying animals
Special feature: the biggest flying animal ever!
Quetzalcoatlus was as tall as a giraffe when standing.

PTERODAUSTRO

Pronunciation: tear-oh-dow-stro
Lived: 125-100 million years ago
Where: South America
Wingspan: 2.5 m
Diet: shellfish
Special feature: long bill filled with hundreds of needle-like teeth, used for straining shellfish out of the sea.

FRAGILE FOSSILS

Pterosaur bones were fragile, so it's rare to find pterosaur fossils, especially complete fossilized skeletons. You're very lucky if you find one!

DSUNGARIPTERUS

Pronunciation: sung-gar-ip-ter-us
Lived: 145-100 million years ago
Where: China
Wingspan: 3 m
Diet: insects, plankton, crabs
Special feature: bony crest along its snout, which may have acted as a rudder when flying.

PTERANODON

Pronunciation: tear-an-oh-don
Lived: 90-70 million years ago
Where: North America
Wingspan: up to 9 m
Diet: fish
Special feature: long pointed crest on the top of its head, used to steer and for display.

ACTIVITY

You have had the good luck to find this pterosaur fossil skull. Which pterosaur does it belong to?

a) Quetzalcoatlus
b) Pteranodon
c) Pterodaustro
d) Dsungaripterus

THE END OF THE DINOSAURS

The dinosaurs lived for more than 170 million years. They were animals with staying power! But their time on Earth came to an end 66 million years ago.

Mexico

ASTEROID

Why did dinosaurs die out? Dinosaur detectives have pieced together the evidence and most agree that they died after the Earth was hit by a huge asteroid – a chunk of rock that orbits the Sun.

The site where the asteroid hit in Mexico.

CRATER

The main evidence is a massive crater just off the coast of Mexico that dates back to 66 million years ago. It's thought that the asteroid measured 10–15 km wide, but it smashed into the Earth so fast that the crater it left is 150 km wide!

MASS EXTINCTION!

The asteroid threw tonnes of debris up into the air, which blocked out some of the Sun's light, killing a lot of plant life. At the same time, the Earth's climate was changing and there were lots of volcanic eruptions. Some animals – including dinosaurs, pterosaurs, ichthyosaurs and plesiosaurs – couldn't cope with the new conditions, and died out. About three quarters of all the animals on Earth died out!

WHAT HAPPENED NEXT?

Other animals survived the disaster. And, in fact, not quite all the dinosaurs died out. Birds are the descendants of a particular type of dinosaur, and today there are 10,000 different kinds.

Look at the birds in your area. Do they remind you of dinosaurs?

Cassowaries are flightless birds and have dinosaur-like claws.

WHEN DID WE ARRIVE ON EARTH?

Human beings only appeared 200,000 years ago – just the blink of an eye compared to the 170 million years that the dinosaurs lived on Earth!

GET DIGGING

Now that you know all about rocks, fossils, dinosaurs and different types of prehistoric creatures, you're ready to go on a dig.

ESSENTIAL KIT
Dinosaur hunters use spades, trowels and brushes to uncover fossil treasure. You have to be patient: it can take many days of careful work to uncover a fossil.

PRACTICAL NO: 8

O tick here

APPROVED

SPOT THE SPOT!
Many places that are good for finding dinosaur fossils look very different from how they appeared when the dinosaurs were alive. Rocky, windswept plains or cold cliff faces were once lush Jurassic forests. So you'll need to use your imagination!

BE A DETECTIVE

How many of these can you spot
in this dinosaur dig?

- ◯ Fossilized dinosaur track
- ◯ Fossilized tail bones
- ◯ Coprolite

PROTECTING FINDS

The fossil finds are protected
with plaster and fabric. Some
of the surrounding rock is
kept, to make damage less
likely. Then the fossils are
taken to a laboratory and the
plaster and rock is removed.

FOSSIL REPAIR

Fossils are easily damaged.
If a piece gets broken off,
it's stored, labelled and
glued back on later.

MARY ANNING

Fossil collector in the 1800s, especially famous for finding fossils of dinosaurs, pterosaurs and marine reptiles on the Jurassic Coast in southern England.

DONG ZHIMING

Chinese dinosaur scientist who has named more species of dinosaur than any other living palaeontologist.

JACK HORNER

US dinosaur scientist, most famous for discovering the dinosaur Maiasaura and advising on the Jurassic Park films. The discovery of Maiasaura proved that dinosaurs cared for their young.

ANUSUYA CHINSAMY-TURAN

South African vertebrate palaeontologist who specializes in fossilized bones and teeth.

HALL OF FAME

ANGELA MILNER

British dinosaur scientist who discovered new species of Baryonyx and proved that the dinosaur Archaeopteryx was a bird.

C C YOUNG

Chinese dinosaur scientist who discovered dozens of dinosaur fossils during the 20th century.

KAREN CHIN

American dinosaur scientist who is one of the world's leading experts in coprolites (fossilized poo).

ROY CHAPMAN ANDREWS

One of the most successful US fossil hunters of the 1900s, well-known for his discovery of dinosaur eggs. He was the director of the American Museum of Natural History.

All of these dinosaur detectives have made amazing fossil discoveries.

EXAMINATION

Now it's time to see how much you have learned.

1 Which of these is a type of sedimentary rock?
a) Marble
b) Granite
c) Sandstone

2 What is coprolite?
a) Fossilized teeth
b) Fossilized dung
c) Dinosaur tracks

3 Which of these dinosaurs had horns on its head?
a) Triceratops
b) Stegosaurus
c) Tyrannosaurus

4 The Mesozoic Era, or the time of the dinosaurs, includes which three Periods?
a) Stone Age, Bronze Age, Iron Age
b) Early, Middle, Late
c) Triassic, Jurassic, Cretaceous

5 Which of these are descendants of the dinosaurs?
a) Bats
b) Lizards
c) Birds

6 What type of animal is a Quetzalcoatlus?
a) Dinosaur
b) Pterosaur
c) Mammal

7 When did the time of the dinosaurs end?
a) 212 million years ago
b) 66 million years ago
c) 22 thousand years ago

8 Which of these dinosaurs was a meat-eater?
a) Tyrannosaurus
b) Stegosaurus
c) Diplodocus

9 During which period was planet Earth hottest and driest?

a) Triassic

b) Jurassic

c) Cretaceous

10 Which of the following are examples of trace fossils?

a) Fossilized mammals

b) Dinosaur tracks

c) Fossilized teeth

11 In which of these rocks would you look for fossils?

a) Sedimentary

b) Igneous

c) Metamorphic

12 What was an ammonite?

a) A sea animal with a spiral shell

b) A small meat-eating mammal

c) A plant-eating dinosaur

13 Which of these animals was not a dinosaur?

a) Ankylosaurus

b) Pterodaustro

c) Triceratops

14 What was Pangea?

a) An enormous continent

b) An enormous dinosaur

c) An enormous pterosaur

DINOSAUR DETECTIVE SCORES

Check your answers at the back of the book and add up your score.

1 to 5 Oops! Get back to the museum and swot up on your dinosaur facts.

6 to 10 You are well on your way to becoming a dinosaur detective.

11 to 15 Top of the class! You could make the next big dinosaur discovery!

DINOSAUR SPEAK

ammonite
An extinct sea creature – ammonite fossils are quite common.

coprolite
Fossilized dung.

Cretaceous Period
From 145 to 66 million years ago. The dinosaurs died out at the end of the Cretaceous.

fossil
The preserved remains of a prehistoric plant or animal.

ichthyosaur
Sea creature from the time of the dinosaurs.

Jurassic Period
From 201 to 145 million years ago.

Mesozoic era
The time of the dinosaurs, including the Triassic, Jurassic and Cretaceous periods.

mosasaur
A type of sea creature from the time of the dinosaurs.

palaeontologist
A scientist who studies the remains of fossilized plants and animals.

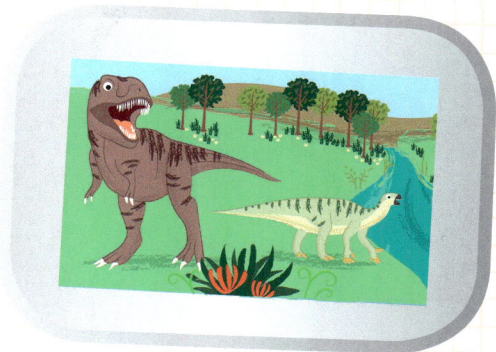

plesiosaur
A type of sea creature from the time of the dinosaurs.

prehistoric
Before written history.

pterosaur
Flying reptile from the time of the dinosaurs.

trace fossil
Fossilized evidence of a prehistoric plant or animal, other than the remains of the plant or animal itself.

DINOSAUR ACADEMY

WELL DONE!

You made it through your Dinosaur Detective training.

Name..

FULLY QUALIFIED

DINOSAUR DETECTIVE

ANSWERS

Page 7

Page 8-9

Page 11

Eoraptor – Triassic
Diplodocus – Jurassic
Iguanodon – Cretaceous

Page 15

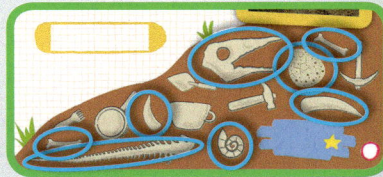

Page 16-17

a = Ankylosaurus
b = Stegosaurus
c = Iguanodon

Page 18

1 = granite
2 = limestone
3 = gneiss

Fossils are found in limestone.

Page 21

Page 22-23

(Sea reptiles are not dinosaurs, so they don't count.)

Page 24

Velociraptor.

Page 27

It is a Microraptor.

Pages 28-29

1 = T-rex
2 = Giganotosaurus
3 = Spinosaurus

Pages 30-31

a) = Stegosaurus
b) = Ankylosaurus
c) = Triceratops

Page 32

Dinosaur poo and dinosaur footprints

Pages 34-35

Ichthyosaur

Page 37

It belongs to c) Pterodaustro

Page 40-41

Pages 44-45

1c. 2b. 3a. 4c. 5c. 6b. 7b. 8a. 9a. 10b. 11a. 12a. 13b. 14a.